A Complete Introduction To Marketing Online

Cam A. Roze

Published by Cam A. Roze, 2023.

A COMPLETE INTRODUCTION TO MARKETING ONLINE

First edition. March 24, 2023.

Written by Cam A. Roze.

Email Marketing For Beginners

The Experiences From Cam A. Roze

Written By: Cam A. Roze

· · · ·

Table of Contents

LEGAL NOTICE

Introduction

Welcome! This guide is everything and anything you ever needed to know about email list building. List building is a popular subject these days, especially in the world of online marketing. So if you are looking for current, up-to-date information you came to just the right place!

* * * *

If you are new to list building, this guide contains everything you need to know to get started in the industry. One of the first questions that pops into people's heads when someone mentions "email list building" is what is it, and why do I need it?

* * * *

The answer is simple. If you plan to grow your business, you need to create subscriber leads. These are leads to people who may be interested in buying your products and services. Most subscriber lists are nothing more than lists of prospects interested in buying the products and services you have to sell.

An email list in purpose is similar to the traditional mailing system used by many businesses decades ago, in as much as that both of them send out publications like newsletters and others to clients and subscribers. The major difference between the two is that in terms of efficiency, the email list fares better.

You can gather leads automatically by creating your website in a way that requires everyone that visits sign up for your newsletter to give you their email address. While you can't force anyone to sign up, you can gently encourage him or her to sign up by showing him or her the benefits of doing so.

• • • •

For example, if you plan to give away a free bonus report for subscribers signing up to your list, let them know that. Tell them how your free bonus will help them succeed or achieve their goals. We'll talk more about this in greater detail later in the book.

• • • •

Back to the purpose of this book. The purpose of this book is to help you learn how to create powerful and effective mailing and subscriber lists (two terms we will use interchangeably). What is the point of these lists?

The point is to encourage people enthusiastically to take advantage of all the benefits you have to offer them through your website. When you build a successful subscriber list, you essentially lay the foundation for a successful business. In general, there are major benefits that one can enjoy once the use of an email list is employed.

When building your business, you will experience many challenges. You may find as Mr. Brinkley suggests, that people oppose you. One of the benefits of an email list is that the list owner has the freedom to choose which data to send to their subcribers. In addition, you can control most aspects of the list like moderating messages, subscribing and unsubscribing people, archiving messages and many other features. You may find the competition fierce. You may find you have to overcome your own fears about success to succeed.

. . . .

You can however, overcome any challenges presented to you with perseverance and strength. Throughout this book you will find many ways of collecting subscriber leads. These leads will prove to be the lifeline of your business. your clients can receive a newsletter, then next week it's a free music video, and then the week after that a free coupon. So let's get started and find out how you can build your subscriber list for pennies on the dollar.

How to Gather Emails for Your List

Gathering and collecting email addresses is not as easy as it sounds. Because of the many scams conducted over the net, many people are reluctant to give away their email addresses or any other personal information. In addition, many people are irritated and annoyed by the many spam mails and messages that flood their inboxes, which makes collecting their email addresses a lot harder. So how do you get past these challenges?

It sometimes happens that your shop will be teeming with customers, and you will have to move from one to the other in quick succession. If this is the case, then asking for their email address and jotting them down in a form is almost impossible. Thus, it would be best if you have a pack of business cards in your pocket, so you could just hand them out after saying thank you. Just make sure that your web address is printed in your business card. Moreover, you can also print your web address on receipts, flyers, leaflets, or any other form that your customers will take home.

Add Sign-up Forms in Your Web Page

• • • •

When the people whom you have given the card to decide to visit your web page, be sure that a sign-up form is available and visible. You must be sure that such form is available on every page of your site. However, you must make sure that they are not too big that they cover majority of the page, unless your guests become annoyed and leave your page.

. . . .

In addition, you can also use pop-ups to inform your guests of signing-up. Make sure that it contains all the necessary information about your email list campaign. Make it look good and professional, too, so that your guests won't click the "X" button immediately.

In addition, you can also have a "Send to Friend" button available, so that your happy clients can share your files to their friends and families. Alternatively, you can add "Share this Article" or "Share" link. These are just some of the ways that you can gather email addresses for your list. There are more ways to do so, and all it takes is a little creativity and resourcefulness on your part.

Marketing and Sales: What is the difference?

Marketing and sales are one of the most important components of a business's survival in the market. While both are dependent on each other many people confuse marketing with sales and vice-versa which is a big mistake. Marketing involves designing a product according to the needs of the market and customers, promoting the product through advertising etc. and setting up a competitive price for the product. Marketing is a platform which drives sales. While on the other hand the sales process is what you do to successfully sell a product and fetch a contract. Sales and marketing together is a part of selling and one cannot do without the other. They can also be called activities. The success of a business is critical to the success of these two important activities.

Marketing is the backbone of a company's future and launching pad for the sales. While the marketing process encompasses the design of the product, advertising etc. the sales process is the execution of all the efforts which involves direct interaction with client either by in-person meeting or cold calls or by networking. But there is always an ongoing rivalry between the two, one claiming dominancy over other. The marketing people say they have an upper hand because they think it is they who designs the products, lays down the strategy and also develops tools essential for sales. They say sales are the outcome of marketing and thus should follow its directions. The sales people might not agree to this view and may be completely opposite in their opinion. They think that it is the sales people who actually sells a product and bring money to the business.

But many experts believe that marketing should play a pivotal role among the two. A successful marketing campaign makes sales easy and makes people believe that it is actually the sales people who are the dominant leaders. The most important role of marketing department is to create opportunities for the sales department. Marketing drives sales and sales drives companies' success. Marketing is like a life support for sales, one who is constantly backing up the sales department and enabling them to successfully deliver the end product. There shouldn't be a race to gain supremacy over another department but a race to win the market and customers working together.

Many businesses combine sales and marketing together but in reality they have different targets. While the sales department is interested in fulfilling the requirements of what the customer asked for, the marketing department is actually busy studying what the market demands. The goal of the marketing department is to foresee how the market will shape up in future. They should envision their product catering to the needs of the market for next few years and be ready to make design changes in their product accordingly.

It is very important that a company integrates their sales and marketing department in a well fashioned manner. It is the correct integration of these two important entities that fuels the growth of a company. The sale people should not be merely treated as the cash collectors. Each department has its own role and should go hand in hand in selling the product of the company and should be the foremost important criteria.

3 Quick And Easy Ways To Build A Profitable Opt In List

You finally realize that you need a good opt-in list. After reading countless articles and sought expert advice and have read many success stories of people creating a small fortune with opt-in lists you finally decide to have one of your own. Then it happens, you think you have known everything there is to know about opt-in lists and have followed their advices to the T and you still weren't able to make a profit.

In fact, you may be losing money. You maybe hiring writers to help you out, or there are some expenses incurred, even if you have a big list, but only a very small percentage actually buys from you, your still losing profit. You'll realize that after a few months when you see your statistics and sales figures.

So what could have gone wrong? Why have others succeeded where you have failed? The most common mistake is that you dived straight right in. You chose a topic where you think could be quite popular and would earn you money. This just not the case. Just because you wrote people from the list doesn't mean they are going to buy instantly.

Here I will offer more advice, for those who have started an opt-in list and have failed, you can rejuvenate your failed venture. For those who are starting, here are three quick and easy ways to build a profitable opt-in list.

First

Get your customers to trust you and your products first. Employing an email list will only cost you around $20 a month. Just launching your opt-in list would not make you an expert and a believable seller. Put many articles first before you start an opt-in list. Write about the topic you know and have started and used for your site. Try to put forums first to gain knowledge about your customers about their wants and needs and target those wants and needs.

Join forums from other sites as well. Provide expert advice and recommendations. When you feel that people trust you already, you will be able to start your own opt-in list. You can build a base as well with other forum users. You can ask them to join your list. Friends are always good customers. Put up a link to your site so that they may be able to see what you're business is all about.

The certain truth is, the money will only come in when the consumers and subscribers believe and trust in you. They want a product or service that could be a good exchange for their money. People are not going to buy something out of your recommendation if they don't know you. A great way to encourage customers to remain on your list is by sending them an email confirming their agreement to subscribe to your list. Then send them a friendly welcoming message. By knowing what your clients and subscribers want, you can come up with different ideas and platforms in order to give them what they came looking for. Remember, if you don't know what your clients want, then you won't be able to give it to them. And if you don't deliver, you might as well say bye-bye to your business.

Second

Find a product or service that people want and need. Although it may not be your forte, if you provide a service and product that you have researched and learned about well, you can carry it on forward. Invest your time, effort and money that you could sell as well as the buyers or subscribers of your opt-in list can use.

While it is true that it is best to sell something that you have interest in, there are not many people who have the same interest as you if you decide to sell something that is not entirely popular or profitable. Do your research well and you would see the profits come in. Also provide your subscribers with promotional material that they could actually use and spread around.

Third

Make friends with other opt-in list users. This is basically beneficial especially if it is someone who has already launched a successful opt-in list. These are people that have the experience in this venture and experience is still the best teacher. While there are many articles available for you in the internet to use, there is nothing like getting a first hand account from someone you trust.

Experienced opt-in list users will be able to tell you what to do and what not to do because they have gone through it. While different situations occur for different people, the general concept can still be very helpful. There are many things to avoid and these people will be able to tell you which ones.

Building a profitable opt-in list don't just happen overnight. There are many preparations and effort to do. Opt-in lists are built from scratch, as your list grows, you should also maintain the quality of your list. Keep it organized and manageable. Get or hire help if need be, just make sure that your subscribers are happy and satisfied and they will be willing to buy from you.

Simple Ways To Build Your List

To win big, you have to start out small, as Demosthenes suggests. Small opportunities will often lead you to great successes. The process of creating a list leads to the potential for greater success and wealth, regardless of the business you are in. In this section we'll talk about some simple tools you can use to build your list. Let's look at each method independently.

• • • •

Sometimes it is best to rely on simple tools and small opportunities when you are just starting out in the industry. You will have much time to grow your business and expand your customer base if you follow the simple steps outlined in this guide. So let's begin first by talking about subscriber leads.

• • • •

Subscriber Leads

One easy way to build your list is by collecting subscriber leads. This is one of the best ways to expand your business. There are many ways to acquire leads, but the best way to collect leads is to gather them automatically, through email or by your website through various forms. In the next few sections of this book, we will go into greater detail about the ways you can grow your subscriber list and maintain your list over time.

• • • •

You will find as you run your business that your subscriber leads prove vital to your businesses success and ability to grow and expand over time.

Opt-In Leads

Like subscriber leads, opt-in leads are a good tool for building your business. Opt-in leads are leads you get when you invite someone to enter their information into your database. When they do this, they are granting you permission to contact them in the future about new products or updates to your site.

. . . .

For example, when you create your website, you can set it up so each person that visits has the choice to sign up for a newsletter or some other type of routine e-mailing. By signing up, visitors are "opting in" to your list. Setting your site up this way allows you to gain visitor's email addresses. While you can never force someone to do what you want them to, this approach often works if you encourage people to sign up by describing all the benefits your site offers. You can then reap the benefits of gaining important subscriber leads.

. . . .

Survey Leads

Another way to produce automatic subscriber leads is by conducting surveys on your website. This is a simple way to increase the number of subscribers to your list. You can place survey ads on your website so they pop up when a customer checks out.

· · · ·

How do you get someone to fill out a survey? It is not as hard as you think. For starters, some people enjoy filling out surveys. For those that don't you can employ some simple tactics to encourage them to offer their information to you. For example, tell your customers what benefits they will reap from filling out your survey. Don't assume your customer's know what benefits they will gain by filling out a survey. You have to tell them.

Maybe they will gain access to your website, which contains thousands of free articles on the topic they are researching. Maybe you will enter them into a contest to win a free gift. Giveaways are a great way to encourage people to sign up for just about anything.

· · · ·

It's funny how quickly people are willing to give up their personal information, including their name, address and email for a gift. We'll talk more about gifts later in this guide.

· · · ·

Make sure you offer them an irresistible reason to fill out your survey. Tell customers how they will profit by signing up. This is a very easy and successful tool marketers use to produce new leads. Most times visitors are willing to offer their email address for a survey. Although your clients will not be able to interact with each other you can still give your subscribers the chance to interact with you by including polls and surveys in your newsletters. This allows you receive valuable feedback that can help you identify ways and means for you to make your business better.

Affiliate Marketing

. . . .

One way you can collect leads for your subscriber list is by affiliating. Affiliating means joining in or offering an affiliate program. When you take part in an affiliate program you immediately realize the benefits of getting leads that an affiliate will create and then forward to you.

Affiliate Marketing is a derivative of Internet marketing where the advertisement publisher gets paid for every customer or sales provided by him. Affiliate marketing is the basic for all other Internet marketing strategies.

In this type of marketing, affiliate management companies, in-house affiliate managers and third party vendors are effectively utilized to use E-mail Marketing, Search Engine Marketing, RRS Capturing and Display Advertising for the success of the product. The web traffic can be traced with the help of a third party or own affiliate programs. A lot of work is involved in this process. At first marketing by this method involved lots of spamming, false advertising, trademark infringement, etc. But, after the invention of complex algorithms and advance security this has been regularized to make it safer for doing business and shopping online. This even led to the better scrutinizing of the terms and conditions by the merchants. Affiliate marketing became more profiting with the opening of more opportunities but at the same time it also increased the competition in marketing.

Due to this pressure in house affiliate programs for merchants became a thing of the past and were replaced by outsourced programs. The companies that offered this service have expert affiliate and network program managers who have various affiliate program management techniques. These affiliate networks have publishers associated with them who help them with the advertising part.

Affiliate marketing was started by cdnow.com who had music oriented websites. They placed list of music albums on their site and they paid others if they put those links in their websites when a visitor bought their album through their site. The first company to link with cdnow.com was Geffen Records.

Two months later, Amazon was offered by a woman that she would sell Amazon's books on her website and she should be paid a certain percentage in return if she sold Amazon's books through her site. They liked the idea and started the Amazon associates program. It was more of a commission program where they received a commission if a visitor clicked their links and banners on other's site and bought anything through it.

Since its invention, the affiliate network has been adopted by various businesses like travel, education, telecom, mobile, gaming, personal finance, retail, and subscription sites, the most common being adult and gambling sectors. In UK alone, affiliate marketing produced £ 2.16 billion.

The compensation methods used are Cost per sale (CPS), Cost per action (CPA), Cost per mile (CPM) and Cost per click (CPC). The first two are the more famous methods today. This is because in CPM and CPC, the visitor which turns up on a particular website might not be the targeted audience and a click would be enough to generate commission. CPS and

CPA have a compulsion that the visitor not only clicks on the link but also buys something or signs up for some service after it which proves that he is among the targeted audience.

Only in the above case the affiliate gets paid. So the affiliate should try to send as much targeted traffic as possible to the advertiser in order to increase his/her returns and for this reason affiliate marketing is also known as performance marketing because it totally depends on the performance of the affiliate. The affiliate team can be differentiated from a sales team from the nature of their jobs. The job of the affiliate team is to drag targeted traffic to a point and from that point it's the job of the sales team to influence the visitor to buy the product or the service.

This is a very effective kind of method because the money is being paid only when results have been achieved. The publisher incurs all the cost except that of initial setup and development of the program, which is incurred by the merchant. Many businesses give credit to this method of marketing for their success.

* * * *

For this process to work you need an opt-in program and an auto responder programmer. We will devote an entire section to auto responders later in this guide. Using these programs you can gather information and instantly send out confirmation emails to new subscribers on your list. Don't worry about having people fill in their address fields or phone number. Most people are hesitant to provide this information, but very willing to provide their email address. There is much less pressure involved when you are collecting email addresses instead of personal information.

Top Two Ways To Profit From Your List

. . . .

Once you start growing your opt-in list, you'll want to ensure it is profitable. There are many ways to go about doing this. You want to make sure all your hard work is for a good cause, so you have to find ways to profit from your list. There are literally dozens of different methods you can employ to achieve results, but two seem to work better than all others.

. . . .

The top two ways to profit from your list are also the easiest, so let's look at them:

. . . .

Build trust and loyalty among your customers

. . . .

Your customers will not buy from you unless you are able to prove your worthiness. So, you have to spend notable time working to build their trust. You can do this many ways. You can join forums that talk about the products or service industry you have an interest in, and look for experts in your field to offer their advice and recommendations to your subscriber list.

. . . .

Also, make sure your website is clear and offers your visitors relevant and important information they will find helpful during their journey. If you are practicing affiliate marketing, and even if you are not, make sure you tested or tried any products you plan to sell so you can provide your subscribers honest reviews of them. This is the #1-way to build trust, and trust always leads to higher profit margins.

. . . .

You should also build a user-friendly website, one that has a navigation bar placed in a prominent location. Make sure you provide your customers with a contact us page and always respond to customer or visitor inquiries within 48 hours if this is possible. The sooner you get back with your visitors, the better reputation you will build.

. . . .

When responding to customer's that contact you through your website, make sure that you remind them to sign up for your free newsletter if they haven't already, which will contain more information on the subject they are looking for. Don't automatically assume they want to be subscribed to your newsletter just because they asked a question on the topic. Tell them what your newsletter offers, and how they can subscribe.

. . . .

When you build trust and loyalty, your customers are also more likely to refer your business to their friends and their family. Some web owners design a page after the order page that allows the customer to input the names and emails of two to three of their friends that might also be interested in your products. This is another simple way to build your list. Make sure you provide them an incentive for checking you out, in the way of a free report, book, checklist or newsletter subscription.

Fulfill your subscriber's needs

Everyone has needs. The whole point of doing business on the web is to fulfill the needs of people surfing the Internet. If you want to make money selling a product or a service, you first have to find out how that product or service will fill your prospect's needs.

• • • •

How will they benefit from the product or service you offer? Have other people benefited? If so, how and why? Providing your customers with this information will help you create a profitable opt-in list, one that will transform visitors into paying customers.

• • • •

One of the simplest ways to tell your customers how you can fulfill their needs is by listing the ways you do this on your landing page, or on another prominent place on your website. People who feel a sense of belongingness in one group tends to stay in that group for longer, if not forever. Make sure you bullet each benefit and explain to the prospect exactly how you plan to serve them, and why your product or service is better than that of the competition.

The more content you provide, the more secure your customer will feel about their purchase. They are also more inclined to believe you are fulfilling a need they have.

* * * *

Let us take a moment to look at the first, trust. Many people fear that building trust among strangers will prove difficult. Realistically speaking, anyone can build trust easily. How do you build trust?

* * * *

First, run a legitimate business that you know something about. Don't try selling aromatherapy to someone just because it is a hot trend. You have to know what you are selling to sell it well. Next, if you want to encourage your customers to buy, offer them some form of guarantee. You can for example, offer them a 90-Day money-back guarantee on any products they use on your site, provided they use the products in the time frame appointed and have a legitimate reason for returning them.

* * * *

Statistics show that even when customers do not feel satisfied with a product they will often not return it because they either (1) forget about it or (2) are too busy to mess with it. Nonetheless, when you build a guarantee into your sale, you put your customer's mind at ease, and they consider their purchase less risky.

* * * *

Lastly, provide your customer's helpful hints and guidelines that will help them get the most benefit from your product. This shows your customer you have a vested interest in helping them succeed. This builds trust and loyalty, and converts subscribers to buyers. That is your goal to begin with.

· · · ·

There are many simple ways to build a list. You can build your list using subscriber leads, opt-in leads, survey leads and through affiliating. When building your list, you want to ensure your list is profitable. The best way to achieve this is by building trust and loyalty among your customers, and by fulfilling your customers needs. If you don't know what your customers needs are, then step back, take a moment and ask. Find out. Survey. Do what you have to. Because if you don't know what your customer needs, you won't know how or what to sell to them.

· · · ·

Lastly, make sure you are always honest and sincere in all your business doings, and you will always make a good impression with customers.

4 Crucial Things You Need To Do To Build your List

. . . .

Online marketing may have developed a sudden surge these past few years, but many in the know how have felt its rise even from way then. As more internet based businesses are put up, the need to develop new marketing skills and knowledge based on this new medium have arisen. More and more marketing strategies are being discovered and developed to cope with the changing face of business the business world.

The demand for online marketing tips and strategies have drastically grown and a new form of business has been born, internet marketing strategies. While there are companies that are all too eager to help your site and business build a clientele for a fee, there also many ways that can spread the word about your sites subsistence in a more cost free way. One of this is Opt-in email marketing, also known as permission marketing.

Opt-in marketing requires the permission of a willing customer to subscribe to your marketing materials, materials that take form in newsletters, catalogs and promotional mailings via e-mail. The more opt-in marketing mail is sent, the more chances there is to bag sales and more sales. To do this, you must build a list of all those who wants to subscribe to your opt-in marketing list.

From your list, you will get your targeted customer, this is a good list since they already have shown interest in what you have to show and sell since they have willingly signed in for your list. These are the people who have liked what they have seen in your site and have decided they want to see more and maybe even purchase what ever product or service your company and site has to offer.

Many people would think that building their lists would take hard work and a lot of time to build and collect names and addresses. This is not so, it takes a bit of patience and some strategies but in doing this list, you open your site and your business to a whole new world of target market. Take the effort to take your business to a new level, if traffic increase and good profits are what you want, an opt-in list will do wonders for your business venture.

There are many sources and articles in the internet available for everyone to read and follow in building a list. Sometimes they may be confusing because there are so many and there different ways. Different groups of people would have different approaches in building an opt-in list, but no matter how diverse many methods are, there are always some crucial things to do to build your list. Here are four of them.

Foremost

Put up a good web form in your site that immediately follows the end of your content. While some may say this is too soon to subscribe for a website visitors application, try to remember that your homepage should provide a quick good impression. If somehow a website visitor finds something that he or she doesn't like and turns them off, they may just forget about signing up.

A good web form for subscribing to an opt-in list is not hard to do. Just write a simple short statement about how they would like to see more and get updated about the site. Then there should be an area where they could put in their names and e-mail address. This web form will automatically save and send you the data's inputted. As more people sign in, your list will be growing.

Secondly

As mentioned in the first tip, make your homepage very, very impressive. You need to have well written articles and descriptions of your site. Depending on what your site is all about, you need to capture your website visitor's fancy. Make your site useful and very easy to use. Do not expect everyone to be tech savvy. Invest in having good programming in your site, make your graphics beautiful but don't over do it.

Don't waste your time making the homepage too overly large megabyte wise. Not all people have dedicated T1 connections, the faster your site gets loaded, the better. Go for a look that borders between simplicity and sophisticated knowledge.

Thirdly

Provide good service and products. A return customer is more likely to bring in more business. Even then and now, a satisfied customer will recommend a business always. Word of mouth and recommendations alone can rake in more business than an expensive ad. As your clientele roster grows so shall your list. With more members on the list, the more people will get to know about what you have new to offer.

Finally

Keep a clean and private list. Never lose the trust your customers have entrusted you. If you provide e-mails to others and they get spammed, many will probably unsubscribe to you. Remember, a good reputation will drive in more traffic and subscribers as well as strengthen the loyalty of your customers.

How To Grab Your Readers Attention With Your Subject

· · · ·

The race for supremacy in the internet based businesses has been really heating up and many sites have been put up to help others to get ahead for a small fee. But there are also ways in which you don't have to pay so much to make yourself a good list of loyal followers. Having a satisfied web traffic and visitors allows you to put up a foundation wherein you can build an opt-in list and make it grow from there.

An opt-in list allows you to provide newsletters to your subscribers with their consent. When people sign up, they know that they will be receiving updates and news from your site and the industry your represent via an e-mail. But that doesn't mean that all of those who subscribe read them at all. Many lists have been built due to an attachment with free software or for a promotional discount and such. Some are not really interested in receiving e-mails from companies and just treat them as waste of cyberspace and delete or trash them without so mush as opening the e-mail and scanning them.

You can change all that. While forwarding an email message is relatively after producing your newsletter. Getting people to open them is not as easy. You don't want to waste all the time and effort used in making the newsletters, you want people to read them and have their interests piqued. Interested enough to go to your website and look around and most especially purchased and acquire your products or services.

One of the numerous ways you can tempt or persuade your subscriber is by providing a well thought out and well written subject. The subject of an email is what is often referred to when a person or a recipient of an email decides whether he or she wants to open or read an e-mail. The subject could easily be regarded as one of the most important aspect of your promotional e-mail.

Your subject must be short and concise. They should provide a summary for the content of the e-mail so that the recipient will have basic knowledge of the content. This is really vital in grabbing the attention of your readers and subscribers. You want your subscriber to be instantly grabbed by your subject and be intrigued to open up your mail. Remember, it is not necessarily true that a subscriber opens up subscribed mails.

A good subject must always be tickling the curiosity of your recipient. It must literally force the recipient to open the mail. A certain emotion must be ignited and get them to open the mail. It is essential to use specific words to get the reaction you need. Keep in mind that the recipient or subscribers spends only a few seconds looking over each subject of the e-mails he receives. You must grab your reader's attention right away.

There are many forms you can use for your subject. You can provide a subject that says your e-mail contains content that teaches them tips and methods on certain topics. An example of this is using keywords and keyword phrases such as, "How to", "tips", "Guides to", Methods in and others like that.

You can also put your subject in a question form. These may include questions like, "Are you sick and tired of your job?" Or "Is your boss always on your case?" Try to stay on the topic that pertains to your site so that you'll know that your subscribers have signed up because they are interested in that topic. This form of subject is very effective because they reach out to your recipients emotions. When they have read the question on your subject, their mind starts answering the question already.

You can also use a subject that commands your reader. Statements such as "Act now and get this once in a lifetime opportunity", or "Double, triple and even quadruple what you are earning in one year". This type of subject deals with the benefits your company provides with your product and services.

You may also use breaking news as your subject to intrigue your subscriber. For example, if you deal with car engine parts you can write in your subject, "Announcing the new engine that uses no gasoline, It runs on water". This creates curiosity with the reader and will lead them to open the mail and read on.

The 3 Things To Avoid When Emailing Your List

. . . .

When you decide to have an opt-in list, it is not just a matter of sending your subscribers your promotional newsletters or catalogs. There are many things to consider in avoiding many complications. While there are so many ways you can make people subscribe to your list, there are also some things you must do to avoid subscribers from wanting to get off from your list.

Aside from that, you also want to avoid any problems with the law and your internet service provider or ISP. There are now many laws and rules that are applied to help protect the privacy of the internet users from spamming and unwanted mails. With the popularity of the electronic mail as a medium for marketing because of the low cost, many company's have seized the opportunity and have flooded many people's e-mail accounts with promotional mail.

But, with an opt-in list, you avoid this annoyance because people subscribe to the list; they want to receive the newsletters and promotional materials. They have consented to being on the list by subscribing themselves, just don't forget to put an unsubscribe feature everytime in your opt-in list so that you avoid any confusion. There may be times when an email account was provided when the real owner didn't want to subscribe.

It is essential that you keep your list clean and manageable. Arrange it by using the many tools and technologies available for your opt-in list. Do not worry; your investment in this marketing strategy is well worth it with all the coverage you will get which will likely be converted into sales then to profit.

Keep yourself and your business out of trouble and potential run-ins with the law and the internet service providers. Keep your operation legit and clean. Your reputation as a legitimate businessman and a legitimate site depends on your being a straight and true marketing strategist. As a tip, here are three things to avoid when emailing your list.

Firstly

Take notice of your unsuccessful sends. These are the e-mails that bounce. Bounced emails, also known as undeliverable messages, are those messages that, for whatever reason, were not successfully received by the intended recipient.

There are bounces that happen or occur because the server was busy at that time but can still be delivered in another time. There are also bounces because the inbox of the recipient is full at that time. There are those bounce messages that are simply undeliverable ever. The reason for this is that it may be an invalid email address, a misspelled email address, or an email address that was abandoned and erased already.

Manage your list by putting markings on those that bounce. Erase an email account from your list so that you have an accurate statistics and records as to how many are actually receiving your mail. You may also want to check the spellings of your email addresses in your list. One common mistake is when an N instead of an M is placed in the .com area.

Secondly

Always provide an unsubscribe feature in your site and an unsubscribe link in your mails. When someone in your list files a request to be unsubscribed, always take that request seriously. If you don't take them off your list and keep sending them your e-mails, you are now sending them spam mail.

When you are reported as a spammer, you and your business can get into a lot of trouble. You can be reported to the authorities and maybe blacklisted by many internet service providers. You will lose a lot of subscribers this way and many more in potential subscribers.

Finally

Do not provide pornographic or shocking and disturbing content in your newsletters. It is hard to decipher the age of the recipient and many complaints may stem from these. Controversial issues also are to be avoided to not be branded by your subscribers. Stick to the nature of your site and business.

Always remember these tips in this article so that you can have a healthy relationship with your subscribers as well as be kept within the boundaries of what is allowed in sending mails to an opt-in list.

Can You Really Use Articles To Build Your List?

• • • •

Getting customers in your site should always be ranked as high as the importance of the quality and the excellence of the product and the services you provide. They should go hand in hand in providing your customers the satisfaction they get in exchange for the money they have paid for them. Customer service should as well be as fantastic so that the customers are provided with the same satisfaction.

One of the ways you can combine marketing and customer service is through opt-in marketing. With an opt-in list you get the opportunity to introduce your site and products on a good time basis. Opt-in marketing strategy is a marketing strategy that is virtually low cost and not time consuming. Here, you get the consent of your website visitors to subscribe to your newsletters and other promotional materials such as catalogs and free promotions.

Opt-in marketing uses your list of subscribers to send e-mail to. These e-mails will contain the materials you will send to your subscribers. It is essential that you present your promotional items in a manner that will catch the interest and the eye of your subscribers to keep them wanting for more. The best way to do this is to provide fun, entertaining and informational articles.

Well written articles full of content and useful information will help in building your list as more subscribers will be enticed your list. When they have read the samples of your contents in your sites, they will be intrigued as to what will come next. Subscribing to your newsletter will offer them a glimpse of what you have to offer next.

Many sites and companies have captured the importance of articles and this also aids in search engine optimization. As more people are heading towards the internet for their information needs, serving the right information to them via articles in your site will increase the flow of your website traffic. With more traffic, the percentage of your sales will grow. More sales turn into more profit.

There have been the rise for the importance of well written, information enriched and keyword packed articles for the content of their site as well as for newsletters. These articles provide the information many are seeking in the internet. If your site has them, more people will be going to your site for information and research.

Well written articles would also boost your sites reputation. If they are filled with many information you will be regarded as well informed and an expert on the subjects that you tackle. Your articles must be well researched so that the people will trust you. When you have gained their trust, they will always come for you for their needs on that subject.

In connection, you must write articles or commission them to tackle subjects that are closely connected with your type of business. If you have a site for a medicine tackling a certain disease, your articles must be about the diseases. Or if you sell materials for home improvements provide articles with those themes. Most articles searched for are tips, guidelines, methods, manuals and such. If you provide these articles to your customers and you have their trust, they will always go to your site for help and advice as well as for your products.

With the loyalty of these customers, they may subscribe to your opt-in list to receive all the information you have. If you provide them with the answers for that need, they will be happy to be receiving your newsletters as well as other promotional materials to keep them well informed. Others may even forward your newsletters to other people when they find a certain article interesting.

You should provide links in your newsletter so that when other people are reading it and wants to read more, they may click on the link and go to your site. With the articles you have in your site that are good, they may decide to sign up as well for your opt-in list. This will build your list and make it bigger.

Make sure to keep your subscribers happy and interested in your newsletters and promotional materials. Keep on posting and writing good articles for your site and newsletter. If you are not interested in writing them or if you just don't have the time, there are many available well experienced and knowledgeable writers available to help you out. This is an investment that will pay for itself in time.

Markrketing – Snail Mail Vs E-mail

It was not too long ago that most people had no internet leave alone e-mail address. But internet brought in a new era that is full of unlimited information. Internet gave birth to electronic mail popularly known as e-mail. E-mail opened new avenues to the world of communication. In the beginning e-mail was only used as another means of communicating with other people for personal or business related matters. Now people of every age group have an e-mail address. But, since past few years its potential for marketing has been exploited to its maximum both in good and as well as bad manner. At the same time who can disregard the services of direct mail which has been operating since nearly two centuries? It is still the preferred method of communication for many people.

E-mail is the cheapest method of communicating available as of this date. The advantage with email is that you can send email to many people at the same time just with the click of a mouse where as in the case of direct mails one has to go through putting letters in envelopes for each and every person, make different address labels, mail it and also have to bear the cost of mailing. Time is money and e-mail marketing saves a lot of time.

While e-mail marketing might look easy but if you compare the net result the story is totally different. When you are marketing through e-mail you go to make sure that you are e-mailing the right person otherwise the e-mail would end up going to junk folder. Also you got to be careful that you don't miss the subject or the body of the e-mail otherwise the net result would be same. In this age of spamming, spammers use variety of subjects, so you have to put the subject keeping in mind that it wouldn't send your e-mail to the spam folder again. In contract the direct mail gets a better treatment. Studies show that direct mail is more efficient and has better success than e-mail.

First, it is not as easy to block direct mail as junk e-mail and secondly the process of blocking mails itself is not automated like e-mail. The other reason why people hate e-mail marketing is due to constant bombarding of e-mails from spammers and illegal marketers from Nigerian money scams to porn to online prescription drugs to stock quotes to what not. In addition to that, you also get promotional offers from big companies and who can ignore phishing these days. Due to all these people have developed a negative perception about e-mail marketing and they simply delete or spam the e-mail if they do not identify it as their regular e-mail. In contrast direct mail is seen with respect and people pick their mail as a daily routine and open them with a priority.

Direct mail has a personal feel attached to it, one of the reasons why people prefer mail greetings over an electronic greeting. It takes time to personalize a direct mail where as an e-mail is instant and the fate of e-mail is also instant i.e. immediate deletion. Researchers are constantly puzzled by the mystery surrounding why people are so enthusiastic about direct mail. But no worries this only good news for the marketers that they have something in their tool kit that works. So marketers have the mailing list of potential customers handy and send some nicely composed letters to them about your company and its products.

Snail mail has a potential of going through the hands of gatekeepers and administrative assistants before actually going to their boss which can end up being thrown in trash. The survival chances are rare unless its subject is business oriented and has some important information. But e-mail wins in this regard, as it reaches directly the person to which it is intended to go, after that its fate is left to the person whether to read or send it to spam folder.

A more scientific explanation of why direct mail is dearer to people than e-mail is the sensory perception of people. A direct mail uses three of the four senses of a person i.e. visual, verbal, listening and touching where as e-mail does not use sense of listening and touching. But this can be achieved by adding appealing graphics, text reading ability and streaming audio to the e-mail.

The statistics show that direct mail has not died and in fact the volume has grown by leaps and bounds in past few decades. A typical example is the fact that we receive more magazines, journals, mails from universities, DVDs etc. than we used to receive few years ago. This leaves the marketers with a dilemma about which method to use. The answer is simple, use email to contact only those people who you know and use direct mail for the people who don't know you.

As Marketers we are told that we should be article marketing

It is how you make money as an affiliate, it is how you promote your websites and it is how you add content to your virtual real estate empire.

Many people find article writing difficult to do because they are not used to writing. If you have the money, it can be outsourced. However, for many people starting out online, money is tight and so they can't afford an outsourcer.

You can get articles written for a couple of dollars, but they are likely to be very poor quality. For a decent 400 to 500 word article you are looking to pay around ten dollars, possibly more depending on the niche and the author.

You can write the articles yourself, and it's not that difficult to do if you follow a system. Many people suffer from writers block or are just not used to writing an article. It can be very daunting to sit down and write if it is something you are not used to.

Nine Steps To Writing Great Articles

Below is a system that works very well, it is one I use myself and you can be writing high quality articles surprisingly quickly with this technique. It really isn't that hard and it enables even the most novice of writers to create decent articles rapidly.

Step 1

Decide upon the niche you are writing in. It should be something you cn find passion in for the sake of easier marketing. If a product isnt presented as a sales pitch, but as an actual product, it no longer will feel like advertising.

Step 2

Determine which keyword(s) you are targeting in your article. Sometimes using tools like SemRush is the best reasearch tool to look into the SEO Keywords that are hot in the month. Sometimes knowing what trends are hitting are the best ways to increase the value for your article going out.

Step 3

Determine the subject your article will be about. You should have a general idea of this in this current stage of writing your email list. You should have an idea of what the niche you chosen is. Usually that is part of the topic of your article marketing.

Step 4

Type into Google some of your keywords and see what problems and issues people are facing in that niche. What do they want to know? What is their pain? What solutions are they looking for? Provide the solutions. Sometimes its best to cross refences between other search engines as well, such as Yandex.

Step 5

Write a powerful, interest building title with your keyword at the start, if possible. The Idea is, the more times a Keyword is used in the Article, the more it will seem you know what you are talking about, and google will like it too. However, the closer you place your keyword to the beginning of the email is the most likely spot for it to be noticed and generate extra interest.

Step 6

Write out four or five short sentences about the problem (don't give away too much... you want your reader to buy). Which should be not too hard. Decide how much you want to elaborate on these sentences.

Step 7

Turn each sentence into more descriptive paragraphs, remembering not to give away too much information. You can give juicy drips through enough of the article without giving away your figurative worms.

Step 8

Write a paragraph introducing the article at the top. You should always have a strong introduction. The Introduction to an article is vital. The idea of the articles introduction is to captivate your reader before the paragraph is up. You've got 3-5 sentences on average.

Step 9

Write a paragraph summarizing what was in the article at the bottom. We usually refer to this paragraph as the conclusion, much like how we would have been taught about essays when we were in secondary school (High School).

And there you have a good quality, unique article that you could spin or just submit to an article directory or use on your website. Content is king on the Internet, and unique content provides you with an edge over the competition.

This method will help you to quickly write articles and it won't be long before you can write a high quality article in under ten minutes. With practice, you will be able to do them in five to seven minutes easily and remember the more articles you have out there, the more you can potentially earn!

How To Avoid Mistakes When Creating Your Subscriber List

We talked about some simple tools you can use to build your subscriber list. There are many possibilities and opportunities to expand your list if you are willing to put in the time and effort. Once you have a solid list, you are positioned to sell your product or service more efficiently on the Web or off the Web.

• • • •

In this chapter we'll look at some more ways of building your subscriber lists. Many people decide to build their mailing list by buying a mailing lists or subscriber lists. There are many places you can rent or buy mailing lists. Generally however, these lists do not work as well as collecting leads on your own. Sometimes buying a list causes problems. For example, many subscribers on these lists are people that didn't want their personal information sold, so they may end up resenting you for contacting them, and even report you for Spam.

• • • •

While you can use these lists and they might work, you have to consider whether the price is worth it as they are very expensive. If you are short on time and have some free capital to spare, you might start with a rented or bought list and then work on building your own subscriber list.

Before we talk more about the steps you should take to build your subscriber list, let's make sure we are clear on what you should NOT do when building your subscriber list. Many newbies fall victim to scams or programs offering free traffic that will boost their sales. Unfortunately many of these programs are nothing more than scams and may end up costing you more money than they make.

. . . .

They can even prevent you from restarting your business and achieving the success you deserve. So let's make sure you do not make these common mistakes.

. . . .

Let's start by looking at some things you should avoid when trying to build your list.

List Building No No's

There are certain things you should never do when trying to build your subscriber list. The #1 mistake list builders make is buying bulk emails. Here is a tip:

NEVER BUY AND SEND BULK EMAIL TO PEOPLE

. . . .

You won't make any money sending bulk emails to people. Why? Because they are garbage. They are worthless. By now you must have done some research on list building or you wouldn't be reading this book. You may see ads that promise thousands of email addresses for less than $50. If you see ads like this, know you are working with a bulk mail company.

• • • •

While having thousands of subscribers would be great, it isn't great if you are getting your names from a bulk mailing list. Bulk companies get their email addresses by using automatic tools, including robots on the Web.

• • • •

If you buy the list, there is a very good chance you are buying a list of names of people that don't want to be advertised to for the product you are offering. You risk being labeled a spammer. If no one asked to subscribe to your mailing list and you send them an email, what are you doing? You are spamming them.

• • • •

Spamming people is the number one way to fail at building your subscriber list. Bulk mailing ads are useless. Avoid them at all costs if you want to run a successful campaign.

• • • •

Bulk mailing lists also are not targeted. Targeted lists are lists that have the names and contact information of people that would have an active interest in buying what it is you have to offer. If you buy a bulk list, you run the risk of trying to sell a female hormonal cream to a man interested in sports gear. Not a good combination.

. . . .

Now let's look at another popular scam used on the web to pull new business owners in and trick them into spending their hard earned money on traffic and list building programs that don't work.

. . . .

Guaranteed Traffic Scam

. . . .

Many new business owners are tempted by offers of "guaranteed" traffic for a very low price. Now, these companies may send 100,000 or more visitors to your website, but you may not get a single subscriber or make a single sale.

. . . .

Why? Traffic is generated by pop up windows appearing on other websites. Your website is loaded into a pop up window. So, someone may be surfing the net and your website pops up below the site he is searching. This results in sending out your website to thousands of untargeted customers. The key to success in list building is creating a list of TARGETED customers.

. . . .

Targeted customers are customers that are most likely to be interested in buying your product. They have, in some way, offered their information and stated that they have an interest in a product. Let's say you sell beauty products. You want a targeted list of consumers, mostly women, interested in buying beauty products on the Web. If you get a list of untargeted customers, your business will go nowhere. Most untargeted customers won't buy anything, and they don't want to be hassled by traffic generating pop ups.

. . . .

Summary

. . . .

In this chapter we learned even more simple tools for building your subscriber lists. Many people use their subscriber list to build their mailing list. While there are many places you can buy mailing lists, you have to look long and hard to find one that is worthwhile. In addition, if you do find one that is worthwhile, it will cost you a LOT of money to buy a list.

. . . .

Most of the advertisements you see that offer cheap lists will not benefit your campaign. Yes, for $39.99 ABC Company may send 100,000 visitors to your site. However, the chances are high these visitors are not targeted. They likely have no interest in your product at all.

. . . .

There are some legitimate companies that do offer targeted lists you can buy, but generally these are very expensive for that reason, and when starting out you probably do not have a lot of capital to spare.

. . . .

That is why it is so important you work on building your own targeted list of subscribers and a targeted mailing list. A targeted list is jam-packed with people eager to hear what it is you have to say and what you have to offer. So make sure you work diligently on creating your own mailing lists. With time, your lists will grow well into the thousands.

Submitting articles to the search engines

Submitting articles to the search engines is a time honored strategy for generating traffic. It has been used since the early days of the Internet and is still an effective traffic generation strategy even in our Web 2.0 times. There are a lot of questions over the best method of submitting articles for maximum traffic and effectiveness. What are the best techniques and which are the most effective?

The first technique is to submit your article to the granddaddy of all article directories, EzineArticles. This site has built a reputation of being the best article directory in town. It is loved by marketers and by readers and most importantly, by Google. It is a source of frustration to many marketers who find it hard to meet the submission guidelines or cope with the timescales for articles to be approved.

However, if you read their guidelines and stick to them, your articles will get through without a hitch. Once they are in Ezinearticles you instantly receive benefits from it. Articles in this directory tend to rank very well in Google, even without backlinks to them. Add in a few backlinks and suddenly you find your articles are ranking in the top ten for moderately competitive keywords. In fact, even without backlinks they can often rank well just because they are on Ezinearticles. Once your article has been published you need to do some simple backlinking to it just to give it that extra boost in the search engines.

Firstly, take your Ezinearticle author RSS feed and submit it to RSS directories. You can either use a tool or do it by hand. If you are doing it by hand, just pick the top ten directories in a Google search and that will be good enough for now. You can always submit to more later on, so make sure you keep track of which ones you have added your feed to.

You can also use one of the many ping sites to ping your article. This does give Ezinearticles a lift, but it also gets your article noticed. Finally, social bookmark your article. Again, you can either use a tool or do it manually. If your article is newsworthy and well written then you can look at adding it to sites such as Digg or Stumbleupon to get further links and traffic.

Of course, there are other article directories out there, but none of them carry the weight of Ezinearticles. Google Knoll is a current contender and is very popular with marketers who are using it to submit their articles too. So far though, these don't seem to be ranking as well as Ezinearticles, but it is a good way to get the Big G to notice your sites.

For the other article directories it is not worth submitting articles manually to them, except maybe the top half a dozen big directories. Many of the rest get so little traffic it is not worthwhile, except for the backlink. Therefore you should either outsource or automate these submissions to free up your time to concentrate on building your business.

If you are submitting articles then you need to make sure they are on Ezinearticles for maximum traffic. Do some simple backlinking to your article and you will easily find your articles ranking well for their keywords and bringing you good traffic.

RSS stands for Really Simple Syndication and is a method of taking content and syndicating it out to multiple sites. It was primarily aimed at newsfeeds and providing content from news sites to other sites. Like many other technologies, it has been hi-jacked by Internet Marketers who have found this is an excellent way to get backlinks. It allows you to syndicate your content to hundreds of other websites at a click of a button, which in turn will boost your site in the search engine rankings.

In order to use RSS syndication, you have to have an RSS feed from your website. The easiest way to do this is to use Wordpress when creating your website. There are ways of making RSS feeds from normal HTML websites, but it is not always as simple as you may think. Quite often it involves a manual process and manual submission of files. However, there are a few websites that will automatically convert HTML to RSS for you. Once you have an RSS feed you need to find some places to submit it. There are two types of site you want to find.

Firstly you are looking for RSS directories. A quick Google will bring up plenty of directories you can use. There is software available you can buy which will automate the submission for you.

Once you have found your directories you want to submit your RSS feeds to them. Manually it isn't the fastest process, but it can be outsourced. You need to have your keywords, a title and sometimes a description prepared, but that won't take long. It is often worth using different descriptions, titles and keywords to ensure each submission is unique. What level of difference this actually makes no one is quite sure, but it does appear to help. If you are manually submitting RSS feeds then you must keep track of which sites you have submitted where. The reason being you don't want to submit the same site more than once. Plus, you are likely to want to submit other sites in the future.

The second type of site is the RSS Aggregator. This is a site which takes a number of RSS feeds and combines them into a single feed or webpage. This single feed can be submitted to RSS directories, further increasing your backlinks.

The RSS aggregator can be useful to mix up your RSS feeds on a topic with feeds from news sites on the same topic. This will provide a higher level of authority and provide more bulk to the content. When using RSS feeds, you need to also remember that many Web 2.0 sites such as Squidoo and many article directories have RSS feeds for the pages you create. These can also be submitted to RSS directories and aggregators in order to further increase links and boost rankings. Your RSS feed submissions will be updated every time you update your webpage. Therefore, if you are regularly adding new content, you can find it syndicated out to many websites very quickly, gaining you backlinks to your site. RSS feeds are a great way to get additional backlinks and to help your sites rank well for their keywords. Use them, enjoy them and see the links flooding in.

• • • •

Who doesn't like a free gift? A sensible way to build your mailing list is to offer a free gift, report, newsletter or other object of value to your visitors when they opt-in to your mailing list. You can create a landing page for example, where customers can immediately download a free gift or report in exchange for their email address. This is a great way to pull in more visitors and transform more visitors into buyers.

• • • •

The key here is making sure whatever it is you offer your customer has real value. You don't want to give away a shoddy product, because they will assume everything else you have to offer is pretty shoddy too. So make sure you invest a little time and effort in your free gift. And be creative.

• • • •

In as much as email list is concerned, a freebie or a giveaway is something that your clients can download for free. The main purpose of a freebie is to get a lot of people to view your site and get them to sign-up. Technically speaking, it is a way to get more traffic into your website, thus increasing sales and profits.

You may for example, offer them a free one hour personal coaching session. Or you may review the first ten pages of their marketing plan and offer advice. Give them something they will value and need, and they will gladly accept your gift and opt-in. You will also build trust and loyalty by doing so. There are many advantages to giving away gifts to your clients. Here are some of them:

It Ensures Results. A give away is almost always sure to get new clients to subscribe or sign--up.

It Works. Once a visitor accepts a freebie, they will need to sign--up in order to download or get it. Most often than not, many people decide to sign--up.

It's Efficient. Once the freebie is ready, all you have to do is send them to your mailing list manager and they will take care of the rest.

It doesn't Require Much. You don't have to be an IT expert in order to send freebies to your clients. Since everything in an email list is automated, you should have no worries about search engine optimization, website design, and other technical stuffs.

Honestly this is one of the best ways to pull people to your website because you are offering them something free. You will get targeted traffic going to your web page with little effort. The best part? You are proving what you have to offer is valuable, so customers are likely to return. And, even if they do not return on their own, you now have their email addresses or other personal information.

· · · ·

Offering Your Ezine

You can also easily build your ezine list by taking advantage of ezine marketing and advertising. For those of you new to this, an ezine is simply an online newsletter. Generally, most ezines sponsor one or more paid advertisements. You can use an ezine to grab your subscriber's attention many ways. The best way is by offering a free or risk free product offer in your ezine ad.

• • • •

When a subscriber clicks on the ad, offer them the choice to opt into your mailing list as an exchange for receiving the free offer. The free offer can be a free report or trial service.

• • • •

This isn't hard selling, just an easy and low pressure way to encourage members of your list to sign up for your mailing list. In exchange they get something free. It's easy to build your ezine list by placing an ad in other ezines that require the user to opt in to your list to receive their free product or service.

The Subscriber Pulling Web Page

You will find there are many ways to create a large subscriber list. As you know, one way you can create a great list is by creating a solid landing page. Let us look at the landing page more deeply now however, so you understand how to design the best landing page possible.

. . . .

A good landing page will, as we mentioned, offer visitors a free gift of some kind. Everyone wants a free gift. The key here is offering something that has value for the customer. If you are selling beauty products and you offer your customer a free shoe, why would they want to opt in to your list? But, if you offer them a sample of your finest moisturizing lotion, there is a very strong possibility they will opt in to your list.

. . . .

Aside from offering something free, you must have your landing page professionally written. A good landing page is much like a sales letter. While you may be looking for subscribers at first and not a hard sale, you should have a page that is good enough to entice your visitors to offer their email addresses. You also want your web page to look good, so if you have to, hire a god web designer to help you build a good looking web page.

When you design a simple web page in this fashion, you have a very high possibility of transforming customers into subscribers. You may find up to 80% of visitors subscribe when you create a great landing page. And, if you are not good at web design or even writing, contract others to do the work for you. Just go to Elance.com [1]and you'll find hundreds of people capable of setting up your page at a reasonable price.

Convert Cold Prospects Into Paying Customers

You can convert a good portion of your new subscribers, the people that have already opted into your list, into paying customers immediately using one simple technique.

• • • •

How do you do that? It's easy. It's called the "One Time Offer". What you need to do is create a one time offer sales landing page between your primary landing page and your thank you page. Historically the one time offer deal has generated the most profits in the online industry.

Here is how the process actually works. Your customer enters your site on your landing page. Your landing page may contain a link for them to sign up for a free gift. They sign up for your free product or gift and opt in to your subscriber list. They are immediately directed to your one time offer page before they go to the thank you page or confirmation page confirming their free gift is sent.

• • • •

Your customer has to go through the one time offer page before they receive their free gift, so you have to make this very clear on your one time offer page. You have to let your

---

1.   http://www.elance.com/

prospect know that this is the ONE time they will be able to take advantage of the offer you present them with. You can start with a simple headline like, "You HAVE to read this before proceeding to the next page to finalize your free gift."

. . . .

What should your one time offer page look like? Your one time offer page should look like any other sales page. You have to reemphasize throughout to your customer that this is a one time offer, so they can only take advantage of the opportunity you plan to present them with this one time. By highlighting this statement, you create a sense of urgency. You want to make the customer feel like it is absolutely essential they take advantage of your one time offer or they will miss out on a life changing opportunity. Your one time offer page should be dynamic, charged with energy and provide multiple calls to action.

Your one time offer will give your prospects the opportunity one to take the offer or say no and two continue to download their free report. It's that simple. You can include the link that says "No Thank You" on the bottom of the page if you want to prevent the prospect from clicking on it immediately without seeing what it is you have to offer.

. . . .

Either way you have gained a new subscriber and have nothing to lose by trying to sell them something right off the bat. You may be surprised to find out how many visitors are willing to buy something after you offer them a free gift. Just make sure you set up your site correctly so if they do order a special one time offer product they still receive their free gift.

. . . .

If your prospect does end up taking advantage of your free offer, you should send them to a different thank you page where they can acquire their products as well as the free report or gift you offered when they opted into your list. Make sure you personalize this message and follow up with your customers to ensure their satisfaction. This will instill loyalty and trust and help you build long-term relationships with your customers.

A more common tool is the use of the free gift. You can create a landing page that offers your visitors a free gift. To receive their free gift, they must enter their email address and name. Remember, your free gift must be something of value to your customers. Make sure it is of high quality, because your clients will rank your site and your reliability based on the quality of the free gift they receive. If you aren't sure what to offer, consider taking a look at the competition. Find out what they are doing. Are they offering free e-books? Free samples? Find a way to provide your visitors with something unique and different. This will help you beat out your competition easily.

. . . .

Another way to build your list and convert visitors into paying customers is by creating a one time offer page. This page should be placed between your landing page and your thank you page. On this page you can let your visitors know about an offer that you are presenting one time only. By creating urgency, you will find you are more likely to win over many customers. Remember when creating all your web pages they should be eye catching, simple and direct. Protect your customers by including a privacy statement.

. . . .

Lastly, don't forget to personalize your messages as much as you can. Add your handwritten signature at the bottom of your pages to encourage your customers to trust you. These are just a few simple ways you can build successful mailing lists and win over new subscribers and paying customers.

Double Opt-In-Lists - What They Are And How You Can Benefit

. . . . .

In the last segment we talked about creating your mailing and subscriber lists. Now we will focus on a new topic, the double opt-in list. What is a double opt-in list? I am glad you asked.

. . . . .

Double Opt-In Lists Defined

A double opt-in list is nothing more than an email newsletter or ezine that allows people to sign up using your web page or by sending an email to the software that manages your opt in list.

. . . . .

Why is that different from an ordinary opt-in list? The difference is anyone who subscribes through a double opt in list must confirm their request to subscribe to your list twice.

. . . . .

The first time a subscriber usually opts in is when they give you their name and email address from a web based form. Once the initial request to join is received, software or your opt-in list management system like Aweber.com [1] sends a confirmation email to the address the person entered as their email address. Users must then confirm their subscription by clicking the link provided in the email to affirm they agree to join your newsletter or ezine.

• • • •

This is why the process is called double opt-in. People literally opt into your list twice. Once as an initial agreement to sign up then again to confirm their desire to be included on your list.

• • • •

Why have people opt-in twice? Many marketers feel this process is mandatory to a business owner's success. The double opt-in list confirms that someone entering his or her email address is genuinely interested in receiving your newsletter or other publication. The extra confirmation also verifies you have the correct email address.

• • • •

By confirming a consumer is really interested in signing up for your list, you can rest assured the chances are very high you are getting high-quality prospects. These are people that are very likely to buy from you in the future because they have a solid interest in what you have to offer.

• • • •

---

1. http://www.aweber.com/

When you don't offer a double opt-in option, a person can go on your website, enter another person's email address and leave. Then the person receiving your confirmation email and following ezines will think they are being spammed, and may report you for spamming.

. . . .

You don't want to upset someone accidentally, so your best bet is to protect your interests and those of your clients by providing the double opt-in list choice.

. . . .

It's also important you confirm people signing up genuinely have an interest in your ezine or newsletter. If they don't you will not sell anything to them. A single opt-in list leaves more opportunity for subscribers that won't respond to your ezines because they will think they are Spam.

Advantages and Disadvantages Of The Double Opt-In

. . . .

The point of an opt-in email list is attracting people to your list that are good, solid prospects. Good prospects are those likely to buy products from you in the future. A double-opt-in list will almost guarantee you get a high quality group of subscribers on your list. This will include people that want to receive the information you have to give.

You may have a smaller list of only 5,000 people if you do a double opt-in list, but chances are very high the people on this list are very eager for the information you have to offer. They are more likely to respond to advertisements posted on your ezine, which may result in more residual income for you.

. . . . .

Having 5,000 high quality prospects is much better than having one million general prospects that may or may not have an interest in your product. You want to spend 80% of your time focusing on prospects that are genuinely interested in what you have to offer. You can spend the remaining 20% on leads that may result in some sales.

. . . . .

The biggest advantage of a double opt-in list is it reduces the number of complaints of Spam your host receives. You don't want to be charged with Spam accusations too often, or major ISP's may ban your domain name. So make sure you always set up a double opt-in list when you can. You can do this easily using most of the common software programs available for mailing ezines and newsletters.

. . . . .

Not sure what these are? Check out Aweber.com. This is a great site that will help you set up an automatic opt-in list. All you have to do is click a button to turn a single opt-in list to a double opt-in list. You don't have to know anything technical about how to set up an email ezine.

• • • •

Another handy site to check out is GetResponse.com. They too offer a double opt-in facility you can use to reduce the likelihood your messages will be considered Spam.

The double opt-in list is a good alternative to the traditional opt-in list for many reasons. The most obvious reason is if a customer chooses to confirm their subscription to your email list, you can rest easy knowing they will not consider your emails Spam. It also prevents the likelihood that someone else may enter your site and enter someone else's information as their own. If someone receives a subscription they did not want, they are more likely to report your actions as Spam, and you want to avoid that at all costs.

Maintaining Your Opt-In List and Subscribers

In the last section we talked about the advantages and disadvantages of having a double opt-in list. Now that you have a firm idea of how to create a good solid subscriber list, it's time to talk about maintaining your lists.

. . . . .

Today there is so much competition on the Web, you have to be aggressive and work hard to keep your customers. Fortunately there are many simple and easy tools you can use to maintain your subscriber list. This section will focus on many tools you can use to succeed. Let's start by reviewing the use of auto responders as a means of keeping in touch with your clients.

. . . .

How To Use Autoresponders

. . . .

One of the best ways to keep in touch with your customers and prospects is by sending out a series of regular and updated auto responders. Remember that it does not write the messages for you. All it does is send your pre--written mails and messages to your clients, and everybody else included in the contacts list you uploaded to your list manager.

．．．．

One good thing about an AutoResponder is that you don't have to be online for it to work. The AutoResponder automatically sends your pre-written messages at the intervals that you chose. For example, if you have ten newsletters ready, then you can choose to send one to every client every day. Thus, your clients will surely get one free newsletter for the next ten days, without you lifting a finger.

．．．．

There are many software companies that offer AutoResponder services. Here are the five most popular companies that you can choose from according to top5autoresponders.com.

．．．．

Online marketing wouldn't succeed today without auto responders. These handy tools allow marketers to contact their prospects, customers and affiliates effortlessly. If you want to keep in touch with your customers and subscribers the best way to do so is by using a paid and professional responder service.

．．．．

An autoresponder is often a primary ingredient of many successful business owners' toolkits. Autoresponders are nothing more than computer generated emails you can send to your affiliates. You can write a dozen at a time, load them into your database or the professional database you are using to manage your leads, then designate a time frame when each should be sent out (weekly, monthly etc).

You can use an auto responder to send out sales messages or to announce new developments in your product line. You can use them to send out special offers to your customers or simply to help provide a means of communication with your customers and establish greater trust and loyalty.

A mailing list and an auto responder often go hand in hand. Once you have your subscriber list, make sure you keep in touch with your subscribers regularly by emailing them. Most marketer email weekly at the very minimum.

You may also create separate lists, one list for paying customers and one list for prospects. You might decide to email your paying customers more frequently because they already bought from you. Once somebody buys from you, it's twice as likely they will buy again. So save your best efforts for paying customers when using auto responders.

· · · ·

Create E-Zines To Maintain Your List

Yet another way to maintain your list of subscribers is to create online newsletters or ezines you freely distribute to your list. These emails are easy to create and provide your customers with a wealth of important and targeted information. You can either automate the process of sending ezines to your subscribers (which I recommend) or send them out manually on a set schedule. What benefits will you enjoy by sending out an ezine? The same benefits you might if you were to send a newsletter to your target audience. You can expand your marketing influence and your knowledge as well as your base of subscribers. You can connect with your subscribers on a down-to-earth level so you get to know them better.

. . . .

This in turn will allow you to offer them products that better serve their needs. The only thing you need to start an ezine is an auto responder and broadcast feature. The broadcast feature allows you to reach out to all subscribers on your list, or just to a select group of subscribers.

. . . .

There are many sites that allow you to easily create ezine or auto responder messages online and send them to your customers. You can choose from various professional looking templates. One of my favorite places is Aweber.com. Here you can create unlimited ezines for all your subscribers.

. . . .

Advantages and Disadvantages of Ezines

The advantages of ezines are obvious. You are able to reach out to your subscribers and encourage them to take an active interest in your products and services. You can use your ezine to build trust and loyalty.

. . . .

However, one disadvantage many people associated with ezines is the work involved in creating an online newsletter. You have to be able to create good content, and that process can be extraordinarily difficult if you are not already a writer, or a writer too busy with other projects. The good news is you can hire someone to create your content for you inexpensively.

•••••

There are many contract sites like Elance.com where freelancers and other professionals post their profiles and bid on projects. You can put your ezine project up for bidding, describing your needs and the content you want, and sit back and watch as dozens of people offer to write your ezine. You will find by going through sites you get very competitive bids, so you will not have to pay too much to create your ezine.

•••••

Another way to tackle the content problem is to create as much content as you can in advance. You can for example, create one month's worth of content and place it in your autoresponder, so in a few days you have prepared all the ezines you need to for an entire month – or even longer if you wish.

•••••

Another place to check out for help when creating ezines is Rentacoder.com.[1] Here you will also find independent contractors capable of taking on your writing projects.

•••••

---

1. http://www.rentacoder.com/

How To Choose An Ezine Topic

• • • •

How do you choose an ezine topic? You should always focus on creating content that is not time sensitive. You want topics that provide universal appeal regardless of the season or time of year. Otherwise someone may receive your autoresponder at the wrong time or place.

• • • •

Things that work well for ezines include quick and simple tips your subscribers can adopt, mini stories your readers can enjoy and interviews with other professionals in the industry. Think of the kinds of subjects you would enjoy reading if you were to read an online newsletter and go from there. A great way to come up with ideas for content is by brainstorming. Just sit down, get out a piece of paper and create a list of a dozen or more topics you might like to talk about. When thinking of great topics, look for those that have a solid market and demand. You should look for topics where a demand always exists for the topic.

Relationships and dating for example are topics that are always in demand, so you can usually create an ezine or product on this subject and generate good income. You may look for a niche within the primary topic category you select to narrow your focus and your target audience.

• • • •

You also want to look for topics that will allow you to create a steady stream of affiliate income by promoting the products and services of others. You can endorse products that you are an affiliate for through your ezine and subscriber list and make a lot of extra residual income.

In a perfect world all lists would maintain themselves. Unfortunately we all live in an imperfect world. That means you do have to put a little effort into maintaining your lists and ensuring your subscribers remain loyal to you.

• • • •

Because the Web is filled with competition and new entrants into the market, you must continually work to not only create but also maintain your lists. There are many simple and effective ways you can maintain your lists.

• • • •

One of the easiest ways to maintain your list with little to no effort is by using an autoresponder. After you have gathered all the email addresses that you can get, you now need to employ the services of a list manager. There are a lot of established providers out there, so choosing among them may be difficult. Autoresponders are automatic email newsletters or emails you can send out to your prospects or customers in an organized fashion. These tools allow you to keep in touch with your clients on a regular basis.

• • • •

Many companies, including Aweber.com, allow you to create enough autoresponder messages to last you a month or more. You can then sit back and watch what happens as your prospects receive their weekly, monthly or even daily messages. The use of email newsletters or ezines is also a good way to maintain your list and keep your prospects up to date on new trends in your industry.

How to Monetize Your List

• • • •

Many successful online entrepreneurs will tell you that "money is in the list." There is nothing truer than this. Many businesses that have taken advantage of email lists were able to get more clients and customers, which meant more income and more profits. Do a bit of googling and you will find hundreds of such success stories in the net. How did they do it? Here are some of the top answers:

• • • •

Promote Your Products

This is one of the most common ways to earn from an email list. If you have a product that you would like to sell but is having a hard time doing so, then an email list can just be the solution. Send you clients emails about your product, making sure to mention that it is unique and what makes it stand out among the other competitors. Asking your long-time customers to give your product a try may be easy, but it can be a real challenge to persuade those who aren't, so will need to work harder and brush up on your sales talk.

Promote a Website

There are many good websites out there, but they don't get the attention that they deserve. If you happen to come across one, take note of it and add its link into your newsletters and announcements.

When you do promote another website, be sure to include all the good things in it. For example, if a website offers a free music download, be sure to mention that in order to encourage your subscribers to pay the site a visit.

• • • •

Sell a Website or a Domain

If you have websites or domains that you would like to sell, an email list can be of help. You can use your email list to advertise about these websites and domains. If you have good marketing skills, then you just make a fortune out of this.

Trade Fairs and Exhibits

Getting a booth in a trade fair or in an exhibit is another way of promoting your business and your email list. Make your booth attractive and professional-- looking or whatever you think will attract potential clients the Bemosuret. that your booth has a theme built around your business, and that forms and flyers are available to hand out to guests and participants.

Target Specific Audiences

One way to build your email list is to target specific audiences. For example, if your business is in line with health and beauty products, then you may want to pay several spas and health clubs in your area a visit.

Privacy Policy

If you want to keep your business thriving, one thing you should always aim for is keeping your clients trust and confidence. One way to do this is by offering a trust and confidentiality policy.

Don't Spam

Once you get into the habit of sending stuff to your clients, and see your revenue increasing by folds, it is easy to forget ethics and be overcome by greed, making you send out more and more emails. One message a day got you far, so sending two must be better. Wrong.

. . . .

There is no faster way to ruin the relationship between you and your client than by flooding their inbox with loads of messages. You would do well by sticking to the number of messages that your clients are used to, unless your subscribers specifically requested for more. Building and maintaining a highly--responsive email list can be quite a challenge, but it is a great way of earning loads and loads of cash if you do it right–from start to finish.

Before you start sending newsletters and other goodies to your clients though, it would be best to ask for their permission first by encouraging them to opt-in for the subscription. This way, your clients won't treat your newsletters and announcements as spam, which they would then send to the recycle bin. Worse, they could block you from sending them anymore subscriptions, thus lessening your pool of clients and subscribers.

After you sent your messages and goodies, be sure to back up all the information related to it. Some mailing list managers can do this for you either for free (as an incentive when you applied) or for a fee. However, you can also do this manually by saving the files you sent in a CD or in a flash drive.

• • • •

Say Thank You

This serves two purposes. One is to say "thank you," and the second is to make sure that you are sending the gifts to the right people. Your thank you also deters people from giving you fake email addresses. After they sign--up and give you their email address, you will send an automatic response to the email address that they provided. The response will not include the gift, but instead a short sweet thank you note. Below the note is a link that leads to the download page. Thus, if they gave you a fake email address, they will not be able to click the link and download the gift.

Provide Link To Related Software (if applicable)

Y ou may want to provide links to download any software required to run your freebie. For example, if you sent an ebook in PDF format, you may want to include a link to help them download a PDF reader.

"What Interests You?" Box

G etting to know what your subscribers want in terms of newsletters can be a tricky task at most, but there are ways to do it. One is by asking them about it whenever they sign up through a checklist. Provide a checklist in the sign up page with a lot of choices. For example, you can make a "what interests you?" box with a couple of choices like arts, tips, events, and so on. Here, they get to tick the boxes of the things that interest them, which serve as your basis for sending them the things that they want.

Mobile Marketing

M obile marketing can be classified into two types based on the technology involved. The more traditional form involves marketing on the move like moving billboards and road shows. The second type refers to marketing on a mobile phone like cell phone. Since the onset of millennium, mobile marketing though cell phone has become very popular. Short message service popularly known as SMS has made marketing by this method a lot easier.

There were some problems in the beginning as unwanted information was being sent to the people. Most of the SMS that were passed around was spam and it received negative media response in all parts of the world. This was because a sector of the advertisers bought list of mobile users and began sending them unsolicited messages. They were later stopped due to strict security measures and laws passed. Marketing industry recognized the potential of mobile marketing and utilized it to the full extent. The mobile service providers coded guidelines and laws. It then became a legal advertising channel. The Mobile Marketing Association and Interactive Advertising Bureau also have laid down guidelines for the proper functioning of mobile marketing.

Mobile marketing has become popular in Asia and Europe as it is a novel idea and in Europe alone hundreds of millions of pounds have been investing in SMS advertising. Now SMS has become the most famous part of mobile marketing. Because of the popularity of short codes, SMSing has become a lot easier. This has created a new approach to reach out to potential customers. Now mobile short codes are looked upon as mobile domain name, by many of the brands around the world, when the customers message the brand at any occasion.

In America, the first SMS short code campaign was started in 2002. SMS containing short codes are easier to send a message with complete information. Short codes are usually numbers that are assigned to mobile operators of a particular location, which they use for brand campaigning and other purposes. They are very small, like they contain only four to five words. These numbers are always under scrutiny by the service provider and each and every message is monitored to see that they do not go against the original service description.

Like opt-in emails, customers have to opt for SMSes. This is the biggest criterion, which the advertiser has to follow in order to send a promotional SMS. Some of the mobile operators ask for double opt-in form from the receiver. At the same time opting out is made easy for the customer. When the customer wishes to terminate receiving messages, they have to send STOP word by SMS. All these guidelines have been laid by the Mobile Marketing Association consumer best practice guidelines and it's a compulsion to follow those by all the marketers who wish to do mobile marketing in America.

Now, service providers have started to provide the option of sending SMS to email addresses. Other than this, other services provided are mobile games, mobile tones etc., which are used for promotional purposes. This has lead to the invention of MMS or Multi-media Message Service, through which short promotional videos and animations can be send.

Bluetooth is another good technology. It started in 2003, and many companies in Europe have found it useful. When a message is send via Bluetooth, the receiver should accept request from the sender. So, sending messages by this method is legitimate. The message transfer speed is high and is also a free service as it is a radio-based technology.

The method of sending SMS advertisement to mobile phone users based on their geographical location is known as Location based service. The customer is tracked via a GPS chip which is built-in the phone. Radiolocation signals from the nearest cell phone towers are used for this purpose.

Mobile marketing follows a very safe marketing strategy, as it is customer opted. The short message sent through this method is known as mobile originated or MO message. If the advertisement is done through a call, the call is known as mobile terminated or MT message. As there is a phenomenal increase in the number of mobile phone users, this kind of marketing is a sure hit.

Write Interesting Subject Lines

• • • •

Do away with the normal and boring subject lines for your emails. The subject lines refer to the titles that appear on their list of emails received. If your subject line does not interest them, then you may find your newsletters deleted without being read.

When writing subject lines, you have to make sure that they sound interesting. A subject line that goes, "Christmas Dinners" is not likely to attract any subscribers, unlike a subject line like: "Great and Easy Christmas Recipes". Research your target market. Know what your target audience wants and what questions they need answers for. Look for the keywords that they use in looking up topics, like "how to…" or "The Advantages of…" and so on.

Disadvantages of using email to sell

Some sales people think using email to sell everything is the best idea. But the truth it is not. It is not a good idea to replace calls with emails when contacting with a potential client. Some people use email to sell products, to avoid the humiliation of rejection. Also the major disadvantage of taking this approach is that there can be a possibility of not getting an email while awaiting a transaction related to a sales process.

More than seventy five percent of the businesses today have replaced calls with emails, and in the process has lost the personal touch. The reason why businesses do this is that feel awkward to face rejection when speaking directly to the customer. It hurts less to hear a no though an email. Some people get tired of hearing the voicemails repeatedly. They think it's a better idea to switch to emails.

When trying to sell products or services to a new client, it is not possible to gain customer's trust through an email, which makes the foundation of a long-term relationship, weak. Some well to do firms, think that they are recognized in the market but they forget that there are strict spam filters installed, these firms take the risk of sending introductory emails to potential customer.

There are very little chances that the customer will receive the email and will read it. But when calling a potential customer, there is a higher probability of the customer receiving the call and all the resources invested will be put good use.

If the company still thinks that sending emails to clients is the best approach, some points should be taken care of. The introductory email contains introduction about the company, brief information about the products and services they offer and information about method of purchase and contact. All the information included in the email should give the impression to the reader that the company is interested in benefiting the customer and not themselves.

The introductory email should sound like it's trying to solve the problems and try to build a strong relationship with the prospective customer. For this the targeted people should be thoroughly studied in order to understand their shortcomings and what wonders they would expect from a particular product. In the first time itself; do not mention that the company and the client is a good match for each other. Sales pitches should be repelled completely.

Don't put the company's name in the heading of the email. When the company's name is included in the heading, the customer gets the impression that profit of the company is its top priority and not interest of the customer. It's a good marketing strategy to include the name of the product being sold, features of the product and how it can solve the problem of the reader. The subject should tell it all, and should also catch the attention in the first glance itself.

Its best to start emailing the customer after the foundation of a strong long-term relationship is laid first. At first the customers should be personally approached. Later when the customer's trust is gained, further dealings can be done through emails. Emails should only act as a back up method of communicating. Take care that word like "we" should be avoided and replaced with the word "you". The customer feels that he is being directly referred too.

There should be no negativity in the matter. This sets the mind of the customer in a negative mood and he will actually get the opposite message. For example, instead of writing 'We don't sell low quality products', write 'We sell high quality products'. Don't condition the customer. This creates a pressure on the customer and they will start to avoid any calls and emails from the company.

Emails can be used during difficult times. Suppose some soreness erupted between the parties or at least from the side of the customer, emails written with polite and gentle words can melt the toughness and can open up good terms again. The best thing is to stop using email as the only way of communicating, completely. Companies that directly reach out to clients reflect higher level of confidence and create a good impression on new customers.

All in All

There are many ways that one can earn money thru the internet these days, and one such way that is widely gaining popularity fast is the email list. Accordingly, it has helped a lot of online entrepreneurs get the clients and subscribers they need and keep them. You too, can be one of these successful online entrepreneurs.

By using an email list, you can increase the number of your potential customers by hundreds in a flash. This is possible by offering them different kinds of freebies that will surely encourage them to sign up for subscription into your site.

Building an email list is quite challenging, but very rewarding in the end. It not only earns you money, but promotes and strengthens your relationship with your clients and subscribers alike.

The success of a business depends largely on the number of loyal and faithful customers who avail of your products and services. Thus, make it a point to keep your community of customers and clients growing – an endeavor that highly-responsive email list can help you with.

About the Author

Cam Roze has been marketing on social media and various other types of marketing to figure all of the secrets to making his current career build and quickly.

About the Publisher